Contents

A terrible illness

It is bad news I am afraid, Mr and Mrs Keller. I fear that Helen will never see or hear again. She is always going to be blind and deaf.

Helen Keller was born on 27 June 1880. She was a happy baby and loved to play. She lived in a comfortable home in a little American town called Tuscumbia. Her parents were very proud of her. But then Helen became ill.

Helen was just 19 months old when the terrible illness made her blind and deaf. Her parents tried to find someone who could help make Helen better, but there was no one. They heard that the waters at a place called Eureka Springs could cure illness. They took Helen there for six weeks. It did no good. Five years passed.

Who can help Helen?

Helen stopped speaking. She got what she wanted by signs. She shivered if she was cold. She shook or nodded her head for 'Yes' and 'No'. She was often very angry and naughty. Her parents did not know what to do.

When Helen was seven, her parents took her to see Dr Alexander Graham Bell. He had invented the telephone and was very famous. Her parents asked him for help.

Poor little girl. My wife is deaf, so I know a little about your problems. Why don't you write to my friend Dr Anagnos at the Perkins Institution for the Blind in Boston? He will find someone to help Helen.

Annie Sullivan arrived on 3 March 1887. She came from a very poor family. When she was just eight her mother died. Annie's eyesight was not good. Her father could not look after her. Annie went to a poorhouse, where very poor children were looked after by officials. Then she went to the Perkins Institution for the Blind.

She was nearly 21 years old when she arrived at the Kellers'.

Hello, I am Annie Sullivan. Dr Anagnos sent me. I am here to help Helen.

Do as you are told!

Because she could not see or hear, Helen was often angry. She did not do what her parents wanted. She ate her food with her fingers. She grabbed food off other people's plates. Annie knew that, first, she had to make Helen behave.

Annie was very strict. She did not let Helen do whatever she wanted. She began her battle with Helen at breakfast. Mr and Mrs Keller left the room to let Annie try to control Helen.

Annie took Helen away to live in a little cottage that was near the Kellers' house. Helen was made to learn that she had to behave. Annie did not let Helen eat any breakfast until she had washed herself, brushed her hair and dressed properly. Once Helen began to behave well they went back to live with Mr and Mrs Keller.

What do words mean?

Annie lived with the Keller family. She spent nearly all her time with Helen. Helen grew to love Annie very much.

Annie had not been trained to deal with all of Helen's problems. She often had to work out her own ways of helping Helen.

Helen can learn new words like this. I stroke her hand in different ways. Each special way stands for a letter. This is called 'sign language'. I am spelling out 'doll' on Helen's hand. But does she understand yet?

Yes, but what is 'doll'? It doesn't mean anything to me.

Annie took Helen to fill her mug with water. The water came from a pump that stood outside the house. Some of the water spilled onto Helen's hand. As it did so Annie spelled 'water' onto Helen's other hand.

Chart explaining sign language.

Oh, I understand. This means 'water'. What I feel on my other hand is water. That is what words are for! They label things. Now I want to know the words for everything. I know Annie is 'teacher'. She thinks I have done so well. I learned 30 words for things even before I went to bed. Annie will be able to tell me so much by strokes on my hand.

Reading and writing

Now she could 'talk' to people, Helen was no longer angry. She learned very quickly because other people 'wrote' on her hand. But how could she learn more for herself without someone to help her?

A Frenchman called Louis Braille had worked out a way that allowed blind people to read. He did this about 50 years before Helen was born so there were books in the 'Braille' that he invented. Instead of printed letters, each page of a Braille book has patterns of raised dots. Each letter has its own pattern. Blind people read by touching the raised dots to feel each letter.

This is the Braille alphabet. Helen learned it very quickly.

a b c d e f g h i

j k l m n o p q

r s t u v w x y z

1 2 3 4 5 6 7 8 9 10

Helen Keller as a child.

Now I can write letters. Dr Anagnos loves my letters. I know I am writing in straight lines because of these raised lines I can feel under my paper.

Helen is amazing. Listen to what she has written. 'Apples have no edges and angles. Apples grow on trees. They grow in orchards.' She is only seven years old, too.

Lo_ad co_al to_ LL doLL hat ha_ll call b_o_ot b_ad good good good-by

Helen's first writing looked like this.

Can I speak too?

As she grew older, Helen walked in the countryside and visited towns. She felt snow and she paddled in the sea. She laughed and she cried. But she did not speak.

Then, one day, Helen learned exciting news. She met Mary Lamson, a woman who had just been to Norway. In Norway, Mary had met a little girl who was blind and deaf. She was called Ragnhild. Helen was amazed to discover that Ragnhild was learning to speak. Now she wanted to learn too.

Annie did not know how to teach Helen to speak. So, in March 1890, Annie took Helen to the Horace Mann School for the Deaf. There, Helen met Sarah Fuller. Sarah was the head of the school. She began to teach Helen.

Helen quickly learned how the sounds of different letters are made. Sarah let Helen feel her face and where her tongue was for different letters. She 'wrote' the letter she was sounding in Helen's hand. Helen soon learned to say whole words, then sentences.

But only Sarah, Annie and Helen's family easily understood her. The sounds she made were odd. When she spoke, someone who understood her had to explain her words to people who did not know her.

Helen grows up

At home Helen was safe. She knew where everything was. Friends took her on visits. When she was nine she went to Niagara Falls. She could not see or hear the water. But she felt the ground shaking.

Annie could not teach Helen everything. Helen needed to go to school. When she was ten she went to a school in the great city of New York. It was called the Wright-Humason School for the Deaf. Helen spent two years there. She visited the city and met a very famous writer called Mark Twain. She even went on a sledge in the snow.

Next, Helen went to the Cambridge School for Young Ladies. This was not a special school for blind or deaf children. There she had to pass many examinations because she wanted to go to college next. She had lessons in lots of subjects, including French and Latin.

Annie went to all of Helen's classes. She 'wrote' whatever the teacher said into Helen's hand. But she was not allowed to help Helen in examinations. Helen had a typewriter on which to write her answers. She read books printed in Braille.

Helen and Annie Sullivan at Radcliffe College.

When Helen was 20, she went to Radcliffe College. She spent four years there. She did very well even though this was not a college for deaf and blind students. She had a very good memory and loved learning. She joined in as much student life as possible.

How can I earn a living?

Annie stayed with Helen. When Annie married John Macy, all three shared a house. Annie helped Helen with all her work.

For about a year, Helen and Annie went on the stage. They appeared in shows in which there were dancers, jugglers, performing animals and other entertainers. Annie spoke about teaching Helen. Helen then talked and answered questions.

Annie and Helen travelled all over America. Helen had lessons from a singing teacher called Charles White. He helped her to speak clearly. People paid to go to meetings to hear Helen speak.

Helen wrote several books. Her first book was about her own life up to the age of 23. She wrote for magazines, too. This earned her money, which she and Annie needed very much.

Helen and Annie went to Hollywood. They met the film stars of the time. They took part in a film about their lives. It was called *Deliverance*, but it did not make much money.

Poster of the film *Deliverance*.

Helen always wanted to help people who were blind and deaf. In 1924 she began to work for the American Foundation for the Blind. She was paid to go to meetings to talk about blind people. In this way she raised a lot of money for the blind.

Life after Annie

Annie had not been well for some time. Her eyes became very painful. Her husband left her. Then she caught a very serious illness. Annie died in 1936.

Helen now needed someone else to help her. For some years a Scots woman, Polly Thomson, worked for her. She went everywhere with Helen. But Helen missed Annie for the rest of her life. It was Annie who had changed Helen's life. Helen loved Annie very much. She wrote a book about Annie called *Teacher*.

Helen reading Braille.

Together, Helen and Polly travelled all over the world. They went to many countries, including Japan, Australia, New Zealand, South Africa, Israel and India. Wherever they went they were made very welcome. Helen used her visits to talk about the need to help blind and deaf people.

Europe

Japan

Australia and New Zealand

South Africa

Israel, Egypt, Syria

India

Helen was a famous person for most of her life. Other famous people wanted to meet her. She knew writers, like Mark Twain, and inventors like Alexander Graham Bell. Sometimes she met the people who were in charge of the countries that she visited.

She always longed for peace in the world. When America joined in the Second World War, she spent a lot of time visiting and trying to help men who had been wounded in the war.

Polly Thomson died in 1960. Now two ladies looked after Helen. By now, Helen was an old lady. When she was 80, the American Government sent her birthday greetings. She died when she was 87 years old.

Films have been made about her. People still remember Helen Keller for she was so brave and did so much good, even though she was blind and deaf. Books have been written about her too. Her home is now a museum.

A timeline of Helen's life

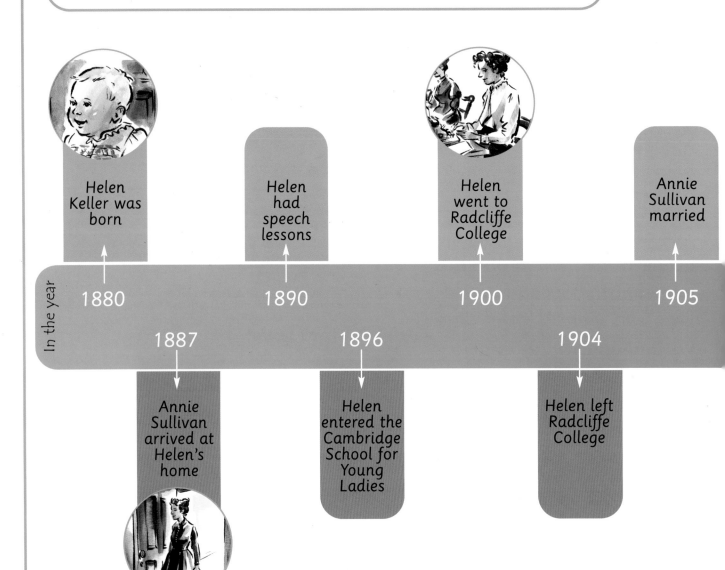

In the year

Helen Keller was born — 1880

Helen had speech lessons — 1890

Helen went to Radcliffe College — 1900

Annie Sullivan married — 1905

1887 — Annie Sullivan arrived at Helen's home

1896 — Helen entered the Cambridge School for Young Ladies

1904 — Helen left Radcliffe College

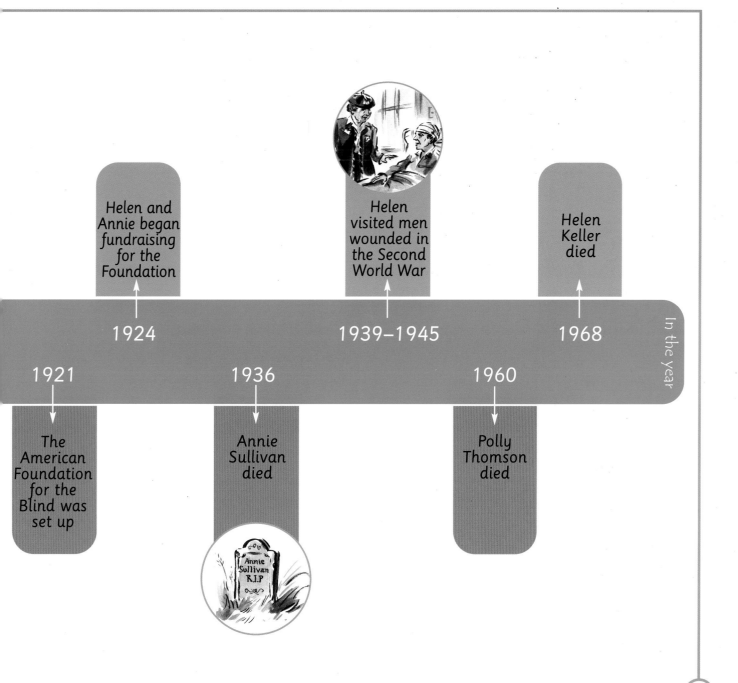

Helen and
Annie began
fundraising
for the
Foundation

Helen
visited men
wounded in
the Second
World War

Helen
Keller
died

1924

1939–1945

1968

In the year

1921

1936

1960

The
American
Foundation
for the
Blind was
set up

Annie
Sullivan
died

Polly
Thomson
died

Annie
Sullivan
R.I.P

Index

More books to read

*Helen and Teacher:
The Story of Helen Keller
and Annie Sullivan Macy*
by Joseph P Lash (Alan Lane, 1980)

Helen Keller
by Dorothy Harrmann
(University of Chicago Press, 1999)

Helen Keller
by Jane Woodhouse
(Heinemann, 1999)

The Story of My Life
by Helen Keller
(Andor, 1902 reprinted 1976)